Everything On You

Overwhelming Love to Fear

Goutam Tukliya

Made with ♥ on the BookLeaf Publishing Platform
www.bookleafpub.in
www.bookleafpub.com

Dedication

The writings here are simply writings, unaccompanied, or perhaps more than one's unsaid, unfelt surroundings—deep unfiltered thoughts leading to excessively tagged roses and rings. It's for one, two, or many; one could melt into the ink, held by it, just unfazed on the shores, on the rocks, or on a jammed flight destined elsewhere, further spilling it—self on self or not, but selves—for no regrets, nor flattery, nor guilt, but dedication.

To all the people I have loved and for whom I have unrestrained gratitude forever, and to all the people I have encountered since—whether in two brains or two hearts, or vice versa—each one continues to guide me through the complexities of disordered alphabetical dedications. Once, there were reasons unlike the ambiguous seasons; thus, the possessions of each are preserved, preferred over many things that are synonymous with nothing.

To people known and unknown, to readers closest and new dearest, I hope I could stitch the book together, regardless of the orders of relatives and the familiarity or unfamiliarity, but it is worth your presence; my gratitude goes to you.

Acknowledgement

As much love as I appreciate and am grateful for each reader's emotions, interpretations, and connections, I feel the same for the special individuals who have been equally involved in every way possible, be it for motivation, staying vigilant to render the pages, or for brewing favorites throughout the writings and fervent nights.

It is obvious that home is always pretty and luxurious, as are both family and friends for helping me in direct or indirect ways to complete the escape of "Everything on you—Overwhelming love or fear," in or out of rooms but not home—"A feeling." To each heart, with all my love: "I hope to stand firm and comply always, to show and gift you all things beautiful, fulfilling your unreal wishes."

To the important guides, friends, and others , I admire and respect your inclusion in molding the once-nowhere desk. To fervent readers, to new friends, and to all I haven't seen through the bioscope or who are yet to be there, I hope you find what you are looking for or, better yet, stumble upon something special if any of your favorites are bold and raised.

To BookLeaf Publishing, immense regards for getting this book initiated and published.

Again, thank you to each of you for being a part of this.

Preface

"Everything on you" would be simple as you would soberly find it difficult to grasp on everything, and when indulged—complex when you hold on to unhealthy indulgence like your own heart or more hearts involved. It would make you feel visceral or missing on some favorites; would take you to otherworldly escapes to compelling nuisance; and the subtitle "Overwhelming love to fear" is the measure of the extent of the possibilities to impossibilities for, your choices causes or changes, and where you're left open with everything you have. You'd feel that reading makes you vulnerable to each experience, yet invulnerable to any if you find yourself outrageous in the corners, but also your own self in truest and favorite pages.

I've been writing this for quite some time now, as eventful as life gets, as we outgrow nights delayed for events. There are a few exaggerations, like if you feel them, but they are for you to understand that dreams are a journey too, albeit isolated somewhere you know, perhaps. In contrast, there are a few bitter experiences you'd want to find solace for; a few sweet springs, sweeter evenings to make your beginnings even sweeter. If you find yourself in a loop, you'd cavort carefree; and these experiences are formidable, heartbreaking, and so indulgent to exhaustion—you'd reread them again for more.

Everything is expressed on different hearts randomly but wholeheartedly, so you too don't feel stuck to one at once. Each story or poetic isolation stands on its own for its peculiarity and for you—your highlights. Each voyage tagged is for a different destination, just like you, based on how you carry it forward, placing yourself in a desired, changing ambiance in your heart, and saying the destination would be worth it, as it couldn't be hidden anywhere.

1. Special box of jars.

We were sudden
not the togetherness,
that bondings emphatic for
life be cherished without,
the goodbyes along the corridors overstepped
be it first-of-a-kind,
or lingers still
that never seen again,
to friendships ever been again
we are here and lost for them;
be it wishes unintentionally etched,
to intentional, the
promises or bands matched,
we are here and lost for them.

Friends more than life over years made,
be in a jar—
confined decoratives to unlike secrets,
then
be in a jar—
restrained narratives and unlike unloved
mistakes,
that we fell on comfort were the
shoulders
failed on discomfort are 'em uneven; but
four walls stretched,
we reunite
similar, memories are jammed too
an entrance, something,
somewhere hidden
to ignite more, the afraid—
what love unsaid,
were we without us,
the best made, but
made better,
the exits handed couldn't measure than shared,
now what remains
breaks and the records
fading on the cards,
the plays unrest and
we are here and lost for them.

2. River to sea, and ocean

Like the seas,
you scare me so,
careless is me,
you carefree
doffing moonlight for dusk till depth;
like the eyes refining about storms
you drown me, or
I say you are the waves
I love anyway and
you don't know the shores, or
I feel you're enticed again,
Mercy!
I feel you,
you detest intensely,
or

you don't love the waters, it
cascades the effulgence, for
love is mere, and we mean,
or
love is mean, and we mere if?
Anyway both the waters same,
alike but afar.

3. Who's half, best, and better friend?

Not the violins
she plays cupid
streams so arrows off the neck,
complicated each
and we, on the table
servings here look stupid and there;
be cute the table's gait
four eyes nuanced so is guide
she is featherweight,
ice on,
we flex the glasses least for,
"Enough is she, overdone?
Plans you and,
episodes to menu?"
We on her recipes wholeheartedly alike if
she carries the set impromptu
so,

love we'd defy bet if,
off the hands likely met if,
or like amongst the many palms are against,
"Are all hitched?"

She owns the miracles,
not candles' wishes,
not our bets on "just likes for" just;
but the total—on the loss too
but her each is vexed quiddity,
the rest for being otherworldly,
and on any extreme here
she would pray insanity for what's the best.

4. Her exaggerated creations.

"Aren't these mountains adorable?
That peak blush for,
she is delighted, so each indulgent do
to that crescent
God......!
So adorable!
She hiked sunset to that moon
effing confusion that,
Where's the peak? So
continues midnight till begins melting all
trails to effulgence;
Steady!
Seems a curve mystique
Steady!

She whispers afar
there's no heavenly physique unsettling else
seems;
then nothing:
nothing,
unparalleled and was a hint
nothing,
serendipity amidst brown and green;
befuddled severe so serene
she meant now then,
and then;
hand in hand,

'em not serenity extreme were
so, she was warm alike
so, sunrise now her eyes
so, exotic she
the luxury shared,
brook to streams
alike her nape intimate glitters
were imitated creatures or glitters too.
She embraced one love
so, all
lovers embraced,
love in verity she was along and no wings for,
seemed vespertine and then the sunset."

5. Favors-The favorites' hearts in nests.

Birds here narrate a song:
"There is she,"
gallery with few, am looked upon hurriedly
decipher a habitat with her,
I am hooked too,
left are tranced
"a breeze euphonious
cliff in her eyes, we spy over miles
she too, we're unparalleled
alike you over miles in sunshine."
Echoes!
Echoes here a whisper through
all prance, disconnected are we a vignette,

"Dawn on her curtain, and
we on a journey dusk till felicity
on your ears, dawn is pretty again,
love by the strings if
wrapped over us,
wings trespassing nests if,"
Wings on me, am stuck for
and her is delicate for
'em cupids and,
we are lookalikes.

If seatherny screams afar,
"day and night
she awaits, shivers our ears apart;
we are amorists such she no extent,
so are you in love transient and more and,
more advent
for where's the heart anytime?
As we carry hearts and heart's still a melancholy."

6. Moments and magics.

The friscalating sun
directing a "set" underneath,
me seeing through your tresses
as it's sinking beneath the sea,
us tracing the consequences
you and me just
so as your lashes cover my sky
so closer and closed
I feel blamed, so do you.

The pauses aren't limited
your escape is dimmed.

I pull you close
just harder you—the sunlight, the other presence;
I kiss your thoughts
your requiting ethereal seems, and
mine aging with wine.
I shall write you the way you want,
mould the way you melt candles
betwixt us, so night be lighter.
Apprise the loves, following
to bide by your artistry,
you being the reasoned conspirer
I shall my love, no traitor;
fall upon me
show me your springs
howsoever trite the night gets, or
overcast the weens, or
cold we get,
I'd hold you,
even the heart.

For the sunset still hasn't,
frayed lashes all over
shading the rainbows all over you—drawn
can't be moon for evasive;
it's you always so,
all the yestreens to,
the sunsets feel never-ending.

7. World in worlds' richest.

Specials are love,
undivided for
always by the clock unmissed
be it overstated or
underwhelming in portion
for the tales since
the senses swayed about the "Magician's
fairyland"
wiser of 'em for the magic unknowns then;
the world still ponders over it
whole-heartedly unless seeing the "world",
in the search—the toys remaining if,
could be it gifted more for;
realms for no exhaustion—all
is more always to that love exhaustion still.

The care—
the worries in cups apart but,
to reprimand tagging for independence
sweetened to wisdom,
excess to reality in the dense breakdowns.

So ever wishes to fruition be evergreen—
"The epitome extreme seen or not,"
revolves that the
vast world in unmatched multiples.

The dependency, or
everything for the sink distant
or unagreed
can't lie to—
an even blink
with or without tears
melancholic,
or affecting the love;
but more the happiness should brim, so
be the cheeks tired but,
not for the love awaiting.

Specials are love,
so are mothers, but—
a word not be exaggerated or,
said at times perhaps.

8. Red sky over you.

Break your heart, if
like never before.
Love,
the rest and more,
but a part extraordinary
like we never met before solely.

Break your heart,
was never to be more;
a stretch, and through
where your heart lies,
still
me past
what the tunnel for, was mistaken
was never for a present
I'm there.

Break your heart:
heart it
didn't belong.
Clouds or eyes,
stay or flitter
are songs about love or more,
whatsoever
whatever the lovers you connected;
the rains are in synchronic,
wherever perhaps,
I wish you love,
to not abundance but
could be a special not again kind;
so not be about the richer.

Break your heart
that was never the same.

9. Magician's cloudland, and a magician.

Sit along, next to me
magic to majesty.
I'll take you across seas,
you wonder where the land skips but;
like a reverie,
you shy off ribs solemnly if
we'll float over the moon
at distant its crater glorified,
or the third eye anyway you
ironically,
so,
I dressed you romantically
houseboat smoldering, 'em inferno

alike mine what carpet and tears whine;
unlike diminished it,
your lashes carrying me poetically, and
I'd love your arms on me now
to wishes this
chest first sea,
you boundary me like a crescent, and
many dipping off you extravagantly but,
effulgence to fantasy,
you amidst you but many asleep if still
tresses to those anklets and waistbands homely,
to not me then a belief even.

I love you chaotically anyhow vespertine.
I'll pour oceans beneath
and you'd drown me,
I'd behold you along endlessly
to wish you surf obsessively.

The sea last where,
ocean such you be oceanic
your eyes to feet,
lovingly I'd call you home
to take me back,
I'd be beloved when,
I see you not across.
or along,
but within.

10. Phases, phrases permanent.

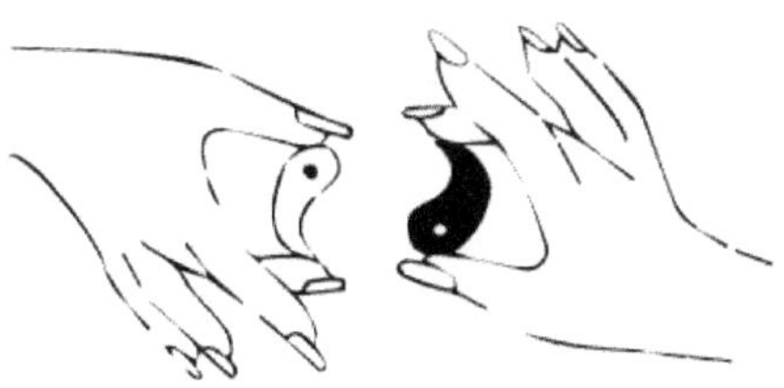

Isn't it lovely?
A moon but so many
somewhere,
white is the moon
are the days overlapping, and
are the crevices;
somewhere
white is the moon
and are the lies.

Somewhere red is the moon
is the breeze
are the clouds overwhelming;
somewhere
red is the moon
is the love so,
is the fear.

Somewhere is the sky
is the space,
are the undefined,
between the fingers to wishes such alike
to hold for grace;
somewhere
is the sky
not the land
nor the waters,
neither the beginnings
nor the world is rest, but
the sky to the space is within.

ii. Raw Relations.

Relations that
home is invulnerable
we for ourselves like
unapologetic no celebrations,
where the life feels exhausted in love than
togetherness over;
not a stand-in worse
is not derided
but a surrounding,
and shoulders over for the wisdom and brain;
for not regrets if
walked or fled in reverse, so
never the unlove,
for hesitation a manipulation emphatic
that say—
why been that the present
past or foreseen,
the ultimate relation be lealty for,
be breaks on forever but always near somehow.

Whether the question—
"A necessity is fair,
if it's love, or traded?"
be the reason itself for—
"Why visceral a relation holds to other resolute"
not unfelt what conveys,
symphony in shambles even
each a melody or gray,
not emotions evasive, but
be for the sinks
love absolute is for
relations left unsaid are, be
it for cradles even.

12. Critical comics.

You wish,

you just wish the gambles authentic were but

you'd never want,

or meet them lone,

united

in a field of live caricatures alike,

'em scratching the boundaries not exits

not depictions—there bragged—

"There are reliefs wanted so,

the beliefs are played here

we are audience too

when someone's to be chased."

You see them unfazed,

often made,

exclaimed for

"Inspired are we,
intelligent inside the box
than all outside"
aim and vain—a pride still;
a few intelligence at the pocket
few through what you intelligible for ordinary if,
that's always white seems, but unlike
clothes off their palette just if smeared but;
they utter "opposites attract" in mirrors,
or wooden rivers and,
"We flow endlessly or
look wealthy for
constant are you, or
them, or
we outside if, then for prophecies satirical be."

13. Vacant bowls in bowl embroidered.

I have written stars
all over my hollowed body,
having smoked the maples
uncompromised blue and yellow,
skin to contrast
even for sucking the now sky is loud
space on wrist transcends orchids in mouth like
to each studded
jade on the chest behemoth.
Have outgrown the sculptured arts
the universe ever gloried,
I have swallowed unseen galaxies within,
lamenting the left for its nothing
I see many on the loose,

am welcomed again until
the tongue sweet and wined calculations,
beyond its expansions
I rest my untamed creations
making it dimensional for me,
alike while rest drawing points to disagree—if no
imitations.

The often led
buried bolides,
I just seek the depth.
Many remain unseen and untold
the ages I fold are molded and kept,
many were never glowed
for the sparks I ever coveted so,
colored are my eyes azure now
the eyelids in air desperate,
unsure,
having stroked self-mazarine
for so I treasure just,
it's mine.

14. Poetic paradoxes.

Poetry is upset.
The world is myth.
As he writes seems all myth, but not
"Don't hurt the author
shelves full of diaries unread
head burdened of dears misread."
Seems thoughts bearer, and
he rhymes "Could heart be two but one?"

I write to him—
"Meticulous, stable without table
more the chairs shared a
game blind"
for still didn't write

"For why unrequited love is love for absence be,
but
the world is brimming with lovers and
unrecognized."

I haunt him dancing in several drawers;
has no secrets unframed
continuous are the nights in wars—not bland
stands in gust, and
ink overpowers knobs in disregard.

He's wary, am carefree for pills;
continues
 "If author escapes, was
he framing a truth
upfront the mirror, or
would confront the unrequited shells.

I haven't seen his golden sands,
nor wisdom on gray mat,
he stands.
There are conflicts and the choices,
so further
"Author is a conflict of choices may,
'em several queued

for the book chosen, each for
the author is an author anywhere."

His often nightmares turn him a saint
just as prayers of each undevoted-a sinner.
Am accused of the quests.
He scours for me,
and I am endless.

15. The midnights' twirls

It slows down—
"The called elegance,"
if wise-
apart body an envious eye.
As likely ever
blinks seem an ecstasy third;
the dust since melding off the heels,
toes vivid of us off palette,
long swinging on inchoated moonbow for,
the perfect grips for being colored.
The floating "you"
or moon burst in rivers by your eyes;
bell to doorstep irked
tempts of solely

us swirling ahead whilst,
the axis at starry night,
along of ascend,
oceanic alike all for "bestow specials,"
gliding the moonlight doffing along.

You,
glimpses,
me, and
entailed are we
for waxing as taken the midnight is young so,
the moon.
Your red slip slithers me then and over
wayward surroundings
waist and shoulders,
the silhouette over smolders around,
such these sunken eyes
the nightingale since selfless,
to you forward
shall the spins around,
around allured caim as you take mine verse.

Off midnight, off trails;
timid nary would betide tamed
to elements over us;
such strings of ballad

to legs and the cadence,
off balance "moon thoughts" so,
hopes romantic for embraces
smitten clocks as lushed,
us being for nights than presence any,
until the midnight's antique so,
we're chasing the vintage for dusks since.

16. Two twos at four.

It's 4,
May be a denial, just may not.
Had the belongings if,
who's what by already
if all nothing,
but that's previous now.
Two at
in exaggerated,
black in attires, attic
ices at manipulation,
feels warmth it is
if not yesterday's coffee brewed and a home;
others on the loose surrounding surrounds
frantic ecstatics
cheering, spilling pot

few stands desolate cheering
pot anyhow.
It could've filled to firmer,
could let in added further
it's up but,
in the air-the love, the unlove
too cold now for
delicate until distinct, and
warm, but an
outside.

It's 4.
Gag—the epitome
scratch for clays made for ages,
got polished, seen
are the textures now unhealthy.
The now rush
not a one to extol,
belongings for
where mean and where meanings,
to now mere, seeming a sentence just.

It's 4,
rise of uncertainty,
sun and to be evasive,
dark or truth

indeed falsifying, to get certainty;
blood in vessel last,
oozing not boiled,
nor to fill if requited even a bit.

It's 4.
Half-naked, half in search
half in composure, but full would seem such
ironic.
"Is it healthy?
Were we together not if two gathered?"

It's 4,
to sound,
where exaggeration lies
the good and the bad,
if it's 2,
about 1 or for 2
louder, where not is moon
that played cupid.
If morning to rise,
or it's already.
It's 4.

17. First and seventh love.

I am on the run
'em not on the move,
love is the poison
is the heart
is the stone,
on the floor,
their fall seventh
still look brilliant and perfect,
remedies on wounds,
are more swords;
am bleared
calling me several, insistent but me for—"how
many?"
Their hobbies learn them informal,
and I am constant.

They call me—killer pretentious,
a circle,
and a beauty spot
I look at them, being on the brinks
them still on the brink,
and tangent is for love dead.

18. Apologies in the crowds.

Faults still on me
I am still for you,
are the reasons for being unapologetic and,
am still on the faults, unapologetic for we're,
you know I never lied imaginations, too
you wrote letters anonymously so,
should you love any
tell me more.

Am still here,
you are still there,
are we not anonymous

on the causeway for across;
I wished were faults firmly over
scarcity or holy
and you the edge perfected imperfect,
to
someday perhaps on the run unwished;
to should you be here
and me there
steady on the move then if,
and
you and me on the cards if,
the weather should turn apocalyptic
but not again against the marks.

19. Dusk till ever chromatic hearts.

Be young,
for these hearts ever be chatoyant;
for wonted since apodictic ever,
and
to it's alright now,
too overwhelming to daft;
that present life amongst thousands,
vista never seemingly
once for indulged were,
lambent if—
to be loved or to
and not.

Be young
when
let the indecisive,
love or not, not for precise;
one we'll ever be,
the raconteurs we'll ever be old for.

Be young,
if never at yestreen so celebrated;
let blabber and drunk.
Once night crumbles pink so,
again if not
would be hearts never within;
the else in lives lost;
to again would fret
"Where do our hearts belong?

Be young for
betraying perfects
you and them,
said be forgotten "Most aren't golds",
enough refulgence to
so rare,
everything treasures gold, but abundance.

Be young
what hysterics don't red then;
so amity,
aren't on regrets;
the childhood if paper boats
not the papers or boats;
and that's perfectly
inchoated, called is a special
transcends the passersby,
and lovers' hesitation so,
them hearts' never old, but
never would or stop too indeed
unlike more, if young and pale.

20. Lovers' Luxuries.

She—
I draw insanity
dithered what those hands arrest,
really seen naked valleys
I compensate edges for amidst, or
she trespasses knowingly
moon, not stars
might lucent be too and then
that them so brazen,
do rain all overwhelmingly;
if apricity
she is tanned for sweet
mine, and her belongings
again, if demented servings
cheeky her
cast but,

am recording these tales so,
her lap
unlike is a waywardness too
she mimics,
wantonly deluge—
I swim duet
taking curves and
she shrouds coat over heart or,
she and, coffee would hold us better perhaps
and her drive for
towns so overdressed then,
through valleys, or
she's near purple and sky—
an enigma for crafted,
her heart's an absolute—
may handcrafted,
she tells love's a dare so,
stares "how to escape her from her like"
stays rainy it, and only shed too
I ruminate God!
That sky winks where and wayward,
spoken the blossoms are her hoops
dramatic tricks like romanticized roses—her
cheeks
nescient the seasons for,
her gushes intrigue a season-orchestral
so senses am on a riverbank if,
she is special of all and am keen.

Her tease,
I note her lips balmy
like breeze in fall-over me, and
when spring candies whenever
charming is her and sugary her traits;
water mint by waist,
color off her feet for river, or
there's an ocean she shares unsaid;
God!!!!!
that collarbone,
she's writing a tale perhaps
or brews inviting so am famished such,
I write the dusk empty, and
dawn reminds that ambrosial nape, and
chest—a goodbye kiss ever so.

Neither bouquet, nor garden exquisite for,
she's a florist so,
for proposing her a rose plenty now;
She on that something
and these pleasing heartbeats,
this heart skips heart and,
I am so pleased ever.

21. What's melodic melancholy?

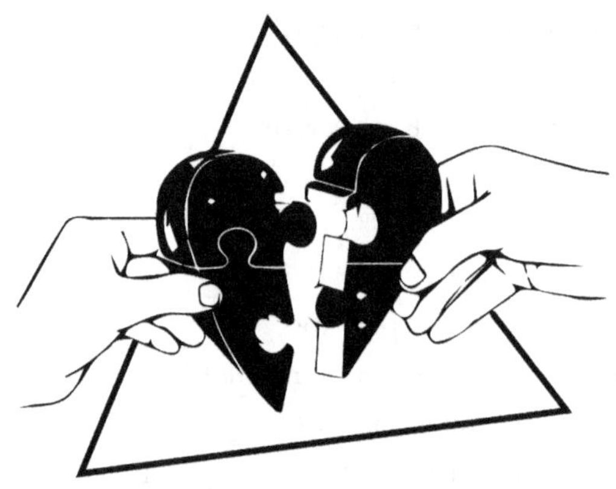

Uneasy nights, or I
say—"You are dramatic."
I rewind her cassettes repeatedly,
she appears vague near me
so, I explain who she is, incessantly.

As far sombre
the drink gets milder always
the extent—
"Please don't,
you're still here,
are you?"

But,
her favorite leisure—hide and seek
on the lips "Can you look at me but?"
on the collectives "Times you wander drunk.
Times been undrunk for the refresh of plays?"

Am aware of bare and
you on the baking,
alike arts around
alike you and misleading for remounts but
"I am sure were lightings off here if,
it's frequent—the switches are cracked.
I am improper when recite,
I hope I'm being polite."

Enough is she, am betraying self since days
"Could you be longer around,
If the recorder breaks down,
I'd feel unsafe like your garden in rain would"
for her redamancy,
she's in oblivion of lavenders,
she loves them so did I countries wide
the cover hurts so do wrinkles
but drowning in her eyes again, and
she is afloat on my tears
I can't stop whatever, she still calls

I miss days for
but not the nights,
the voices don't tremble in volumes anyway,
the scenes nor speak
the flawed box of finest art.

"You are safe,
am stuck to waters for,
you are more than it and combined, and
I hope if could
I emerge, to all at rest
last dance or vain—
the remorse and you last."

22. Grays and Silvers.

Silver lining on the sleeves
any nights'd be magnified for,
whether the eyes
or the linings, surroundings so,
been on clouds—gray, or
heart
redder than a droplet
falls on the ribs unhurriedly when
stays gray not silver,
but since the sleeves so,
silver are the stitches on black
been a thread loose then,
or to constellations stuck on an eclipse too now
like doesn't matter—white and the blues.

The inquisitions for
"Gold sucked in the attire?"
answering itself without the attic and satire;

There were golden back
arm without sleeves, or
lips-knife not for beliefs;
the plate, or
food of the god so;
now the silver at the brink the
spoon, or
the lining one could think.
There are and
were loves so,
not everything was love but—"Extremes
disguised,"
and then are and were extremes so golden,
should be for,
silver on them.

23. Unfair sayings, or unsaid?

Uncertain over us for,
nights fall short where, and chaotic?
The lights turn off the moon when
we gather at the moon when,
should the secrets your—glared upon then, or
intentional were but the then "suffering secrecies
since,"
and everything lost yet found—
"A moon in a crevice enlarged,"
will we all meet ever,
without the moon?

Transcending
the agony,

the lament of loners if,
the surface without
the sun,
the stars not at cusp of "shooting themselves
sable"
the safe is just ceiling or terrace at fortnights
will we all meet ever,
without the moon?

24. Twin Textured Hearts

What if all,
about hearts in a mold valiant
and vain,
pictured assertively, and
you're opaque and rest glass only,
not to be seen—"Famous spotlight for
certainties?"

As transparent the uncertainties over,
twin glasses on the ironies, but symmetrical
one shines on you for,
the rest in pieces
or polished for you, and ones—
in love,
out of love,
everything isn't love, and
you're left with the bluff or verse.

Echoes opacity—
"What's all?If nothing" on the stolen tape,
opacity be the unreplaced, unfilled glass
echoes within 'em—
"Is everything worth, if priceless is any of two
crystals?"

25. Something, and something.

Call me a poet, or
call me a painter,

dense in the abstract crossroads for, or
abstract in the dense crossroads

"Could you write me every day,
ethereal,
extraordinary at escapes,
embellished like writers' ink and vape,
enticed way nothing could break the heart
mourn
on the pages, tarnish since what's beloved known
on the books, ever revered loved stories to torn,

thinking of self in other's space,
life in exceptional than life in the mist
alike,
but possible,
everything is chimerical but worn?"

"Could you paint me unreal,
uncertain,
unwavering on the mountains coloring it,
glancing at the window decorating it,
running with the streams—tea pouring it,
plucking the daisies overflowing me—limit,
sharing the birds—recitals
language kissing albeit,
watering the roses but I am redder over when we
meet
like everything around,
but all revolve a king?"

Writing on the blossoms would fade,
painting on the blossoms that's shade;
or,
writing on the blossom is time's antique,
painting on the blossom is seers' critique.

Beauty lies in the eyes of the beholder, and
beauty lies in the eyes of the beholder.

So could you be,
a blob unkempt swaying, or
to a canvas self
or,
are a paper tarnishing hands, or
to a board in the mines.

9 789363 305441